UNDERWORLDS

Also by Patrick Sylvain

Poetry written in Haitian Creole
Mazakwa: 1492-1992
Zanzèt
Zèl Papiyon
Masuife

Poetry in Haitian and English
Lanmou, Anvi, Pèdans // Love, Loss, Lust

Play in Haitian Creole
Twokèt Lavi

Short Story
Maryaj Ide ak Imajinasyon

Novel
Anba Bòt Kwokodil

UNDERWORLDS

poems

Patrick Sylvain

CENTRAL SQUARE PRESS

Copyright © 2018 by Patrick Sylvain.

All rights reserved. No part of this book may be used or reproduced in any manner whatsoever without written permission from the publisher, except in the case of brief quotations embodied in critical articles or reviews.

All inquiries and permissions requests should be addressed to the Publisher:

Central Square Press
Lynn, Massachusetts

publisher@centralsquarepress.com
www.centralsquarepress.com

Printed in the United States of America
First Edition

ISBN-13: 978-1-941604-07-6

ISBN-10: 1-941604-07-2

Cover art: "The Unfurling" by Renold Laurent

Book design: Enzo Silon Surin

*For
Jalene,
Kamil,
Menelik*

To the ancestors who fought and died for freedom

CONTENTS

Part One

"Discovery"	3
Atlantic Souls	4
History of Laments	5
Caravels and Gunboats	7
A Naked State	8
A State of Occupation	9

Part Two

A Palace of Mourners	14
Survey at Body #33	16
Granulated Hopes	18
The Coffin Maker & The Poet	21
A State of Encounter	26
An Unimmaculate State	28
Substance	30
Howling Wind	31
Acknowledgments	32
About the Author	33

underworlds

Part One

"the lantern of a caravel,
and that was Genesis.
Then there were the packed cries,
the shit, the moaning"

—Derek Walcott, "The Sea is History"

"Discovery"

Far beyond the Caribbean Sea, swift
As a sailfish, the word "discovery" sped by
Scattering fishhooks and death—gills
Pried open for gold, tongues tasting briny swords.

Salt on wounds, wounds salted. A new world
For salt, spices. Seasoned paradise fashioned
By castled minds. Mines and cane fields
Morphed paradise into cemeteries of dreams.

Speeding swiftly beyond the Caribbean
Sea, Taino babies burst like tomatoes
At the tips of conquistadors' swords—"discovery".
Bipedal sea anemones with venom-filled tentacles.

They brought orgies of violence. Scattering severed hands
Like dead branches at mine entrances, no longer
Able to grasp the hands of their lovers. As gold
Adorned fingers scribed saintly new names given

To islands burning under molten lead—
Homage paid to a foreign, blood thirsty God.
Madness run amok, black souls are permanent loots
Entangled in cheap labor like netted Red Snappers.

Atlantic Souls

For the loved ones

Ethereal graveyards lie in the depths of the Atlantic,
Where bleached bones anchor crossroads,
Silver swords, gold coins, and iron chains,
Unable to outstrip the darkness of the leviathan.

I close my eyes to hear an orchestra of waves battering
Honeycomb-like rocks on the edge of land. This is where
Sterns incessantly sliced waves, bringing in bound feet,
The bulk of tattered beings salted and assaulted to nothingness.

I am a vessel, unseen, sailing through night's wet curtain,
And comfortable beyond the brim of light. Wind
Stirs me homeward to latitude zero, where I hear
The songs of the unnumbered and the unbaptized.

Sometimes I take to the sky with outcast seagulls,
Venting pain in distressed shrieks, grieving drowned
Musical hearts. Singing to the goddesses of the sea, and pleading
The breaking of leviathan's lingering trade of coastal mariners.

In the depths of the Atlantic, there are ethereal graveyards.
Clusters of entwined families humming in the confinement
Of the sea. Through gaunt hopes, their quiescent souls
Channel flecks of flames of the ancestral phoenixes.

History of Laments

The ocean twitches in limbs,
Cuts loose shipwrecks in our veins.
Millions entombed.
The clattering clinks of history.
And we cruise the Atlantic, island hopping.
It is not the jangle of the chains,
But the lives scattered, cluttered in clusters
Across a bleeding continent. Work angels linked
To lines of unending fluencies, nourishing
Towers to sphere influence. Algorithms
Brace skyscrapers where gold
And diamonds burn desires of Ponziers.

I sheathe myself with the memories of the
Choctaw, Taïnos, Arawaks and Yorubas—
Morphing my abode into a swift bayonet
Of a temple. Our backs cannot remain
A coveted trampoline—lives trampled
Upon for centuries, absent of conscience—
Now silence prevails as if the past is vaulted
In the void: unspeakable domes of bones.

Regardless of bible thumping and trumpet
Blaring for a blessed providence, we hear
The clanking chains. Skeletons
Framed structures of success. Crossbeams,
Memories forming transversal recollections.

The genesis of your market, Wall Street,
Is imprinted on our sugar-crushed-backs.
My pen bleeds in a sea of lost
Reminiscences, a bricolage of dead hopes.
Through fragmentary lines, I try to stitch
Patches of poetry from ancestral tongues
Refusing to reveal their succumbed brutalities.
I am committed to un-scab the past with
A fountain pen until Atlantic's water spirits
Lament in harmonic disemboweling squeals.

Caravels and Gunboats

For us, the survivors

I've watched caravels allegorically anchor
Into ports and row in sorrow on violent waves.
Memories are crackling with blades of canes
And lash whips the way that shells crack
On edgy rocks so children can remember the bittersweet
Taste of freedom measured on banknotes.

If only our archipelago could speak of thousands of shipwrecks,
The millions of Tainos swooped by Columbus' sword,
The great corals and the wild orchids flattened for beds of sugar
And coffee that suffused planting into our blood.
Terrorism is not new; the people of *Terra Incognita* felt the orgy
Of blades the way Santa Maria's bow sliced placid seas.

This archipelago has known an allogamy of violence,
Liberty plucked from *Terra L'Ouverture's* nascent socket,
Whipped bodies shuddered as freedom oozed on the new plantation
Of misery—caravels morphed into gunboats, our eyes grieved
The medley of canon balls—forgetting that a giant palm tree
Is an easy target in a field of bent backs and crowned shrubs.

Terrorism is not new for the people of *Terra Incognita*,
Grandpa said Maria was not a Santa; neither was Roosevelt.
Caravels and gunboats allegorically anchored into ports
As days merged into nights of sorrow, and the upshot of labor
Foamed at the mouth. Anguish scaled our faces as the clamor
Of the ports and the livestock silenced our bereaving cells.

A Naked State

Children around here show their rotten teeth.
When someone asks me for my age; they know
I don't know under which president I was born.
But, I was a little one when the Americans left.
My father was a rag doll in their bayonets.

What I can tell you is, I am old and unwanted.
I'll die homeless in my homeland, wearing
The smell of the earth like an animal's skin. Maybe,
I am an animal! I sleep on porches, on benches,
And beside the hut near the cotton-silk tree.

Sorry for my smell, but I am my own house, and I
Breathe the agony that I wear—the malaise of other
Paupers who get to sleep on straw mats behind
Closed wooden doors too heavy for their frames.
I am the curse and the source of prickly laughter.

My name is Cyncil Saint-Cillien, but they call me
Santi chien, or dog-smell, and I accept it as my new
Baptismal name, one that matches my animal state.
There are times they called me *moun fou*, crazy man,
I dance for them while the fragrance of their food slaps

My nostrils, and I swing away from a poor man's death.
Hunger killed my pride many moons after Papa Doc's
Militiamen wolfed my family and burned my house down.
I've grown accustomed to dwelling in decay and ridicule.
I'll dance to my grave, despite the iron chain of poverty.

A State of Occupation

(U.S. Occupation of Haiti: 1915-1934)

1
Before the dawn of July nineteen-fifteen, the ocean
Waves moaned the weight of the iron sharks
Faring marines like storms approaching the Haitian
Shores. As wind whimpered through avocado trees,
And the engines roared toward the absent prince's
Port of Port-au-Prince, the frigates and the pelicans
Shrieked their warnings so vigils could be kept, and
Doors locked against the descendants of Columbus,
Who took for themselves Amerigo Vespucci's name
Given to two continents as if Monroe was an absolute
Guardian doctrinaire of the Americas. And you, Major
General Butler, spearheaded the new pillage of an old
Colony with stanzas of gold in its national bank coffer.
The bow of your ship, USS Connecticut, sliced through
Waves as sharp as a blade. Your 5th and 13th regiments
Touched another soil, soiling sovereignty for capital.

2
Dear Major General Butler and Admiral Caperton,
Haiti was a night light flickering out against chaotic
Winds, and your American hands were the perfect
Parawinds. The gentle giant who only stepped in
To provide order. Haiti was a land of bandits. A land
Of political marauders that had to be brought into line.

A line of civility where French speaking niggers would
Learn the southern etiquettes of Jim Crow coquetries.
The black man was nothing to you but a commodity,
Chattel labor with no will to sing his own songs beyond
His designated cage that was formulated by Columbus'
Progeny. They tinkered with servitude and slavery, made
Capitalism God's providence, and the white man
Guardian of the eternal spring of dolled-up tyranny.
Charlemagne Péralte and his men, the wretched
Inheritors of the earth, smelled the leaves of trickery.

3
These men who formed the resistance were called
Cacos. Black chested men with blood stained shoulders
Like the crying caco bird. Black and red. Blackness
Of the night made them weightless, birds with silent
Wings that fluttered in the white man's imagination.
But you, your officers, and your regiments, practiced
Warfare like the intake of breaths. Killing was a sniff.
A way of tricking sons and daughters into informants,
Bribing so your swords would minimize the red stains stacked
Inside the sheaths. You succeeded in knowing how black
Shadows walked without stirring the grass and blending in
With the foliage. You succeeded by turning neighbors into
National venom, accomplices in a kinsman's death. So,
It was that Jean-Baptiste Conzé, a northern businessman
From Grand Rivière, greedy for more capital, who aided Captain
Herman Hanneken like a pimp's whore in capturing Péralte.

4
Before Black-face was a staple of Broadway and Hollywood,
Captain Hanneken adorned a black-face with peasant garb,
And ammunition in burlap sacks. His Gendarmerie soldiers,
Black Haitians, also disguised, pursuing Charlemagne Péralte
Through the wooded mountains like mongoose hunting snakes.
Jean-Baptiste Conzé made the Captain a better trickster, aided
By private François, Conzé's secretary, who became a trusted
Laissez-passer, accessed the confined outpost of Péralte like
A brother. There were no wrinkles in the embroidered plan.
With Hanneken's oil-painted skin, and the cover of the night,
He became a dark lord with his Colt 45 loaded with leaded
Azraels. Lieutenant William Button, the black-faced twin
Of the Captain armed with a machine gun, stood fifteen feet
From Péralte. Back turned near a campfire, talking to his wife
About the mammoth attack on Grand Rivière. Confident
Of his fellow Cacos, he knew he would blaze another path.

5
Freedom never came. Treasons flared out of muzzles,
Making angels of death flutter like humming birds.
Hanneken's bullets pierced Péralte's heart, while Lieutenant
Button sprayed the outpost as if overtaken by an invasion
Of vampire bats and fireflies. The night of the thirty-first
Of October broke the Cacos' wings. Péralte, roped to a wooden
Door like a prized shark, was paraded like an unmasked demon.
A contained plague. Demoralized and leaderless, most of Péralte's
Fighters (whom you called bandits), became suspicious of their
Comrades. They put down their swords and carabines to return

To the farms. With hoes, axes, and machetes, they cultivated
Crops for the international market while beading prayer beads
For an agreeable living. You Major Butler, Captain Hanneken,
Lieutenant Button, and others have multiplied the pins on your chests,
The shoulder stripes, and heroic medal counts, as the dead Haitian
Peasants, the niggers, who dared dreaming of freedom, mounted.

6

As peasant bodies departed from their Caco souls, the corvée,
Took on Jim Crow-like stature. Bent black bodies chained
In hordes of gangs, broke rocks, cleared bushes, paved roads,
Laid beams for the railroad tracks carrying sugar cane.
Nine thousand men strong-armed to work on a 170-mile unpaved
Highway without receiving a dime. A "trade-off" for not paying taxes.
Northern and southern Haiti linked by commerce, and Cacoism
Silenced in the graveyard of history. You declared your love
For Haiti: pushing a shotgun constitution that favored U.S. ownership.
After all, the best houses in Port-au-Prince were arrogated
For the officers, and you prowled in a ginger bread house with wide
Verandas, a shaded garden, and eight servants to do your bidding.
As for us, the caco birds tirelessly cried to defend our nests, but
The seeds of our suffering were plumed with colonial straightjackets,
We have fashioned crooked saplings devoid of L'Ouverture,
Dessalines, or Péralte genes, mostly Conzés are germinating.

Part Two

"Following the sailor's murder, the planters hung two men of color as an example. Though they swore they had been mere innocent bystanders, they were brought to the public square and hung from lampposts after a mockery of a trial."

—Marie Vieux-Chauvet
(*Dance on the Volcano*. {1957} 2016; Tr. Kaiama L. Glover)

"What a remarkable thing a voice is—
In Haiti the poor gather to protest in the slum of Cité Soleil, but no one is smiling at the irony."

—Chris Abani (*Sanctificum*, 2010)

A Palace of Mourners

I sought to shield and suppress
Memories from surfacing,
Houdinies escaped
From opaque brain cells that harbored
A palace of mourners. In the country of my birth,
Nightsticks have swung from Columbus
To modern leaders, while nefarious
Passions have cooked fear into our psyche.

After nights of memories poking needles in my sleep,
Floods of images breached the silence of my pen.
Joseph, a 26 year-old journalist, arrested in August of '92,
Demanded to speak. My head became an echo chamber
Where tales of the dead and brutalized reverberated.
Their screams, exploding the corral of memories,
Formed a tapestry: Joseph's blistered backside,
Broken right knee, and cicatrized head.

The army wanted to teach him
The language of silence.
Thin, glowing wires
Turned his tongue into an eel,
Slapping words to incomprehension.
Still, he did not swallow fear or confess.
He trumpeted justice despite his scars
And inability to move bowels.

Even with this carnival of nightsticks
And stench, I've desperately tried to write
About the movement of clouds and pastoral images,
But screams and agonies of a valley of Haitians
Ferociously migrating to the center
Of my pastoral scenes have torn up
The white lilies and the dandelions.
Instead of flowers, my pen bled an agonizing nation.

Survey at Body #33

For Jean-Marc Paillant (1956-2010)
January 2010 Earthquake, Haiti

His brand new car, metallic blue, waiting
For his return. His quickened steps
To the second floor of his ex-wife's home
Brought dust in, on his black shoes—
Later removed and stolen.

His sealed mouth never revealed
The taste of billowing earth, nor his screams
For mercy. His life evaporated
On the dojo of poverty
The way hot air vaporizes water
On those unmerciful streets.

I've walked those streets, once lined
With palms and flowers, now sepulchral
With unwanted bloated bodies.
A bloated nation made junk,
And skunking the air with corruption.
Even microbes and insects grow full.

Cousin Jonas, an angiographic poem is my lament
For the pus-laden bodies ceasing to bleed.
That January afternoon, the earth drum-rolled
A discord underneath innocent feet,

Becoming a macabre marching band cloaking joy,
And choking the national anthem to moans.
The Palace lay gutted and twisted, as you were,
Dumped into a common grave, now sprouting wild grass.

Granulated Hopes

I
It was still daylight as peddlers' feet hurried
Toward rest where dependent mouths
Awaited meager meals. Desperate.
For laborers, it was near the end of a harsh day,
Tilling the earth shirtless, barefoot, calloused
Hands armed with century old sickles and hoes.

II
Unadorned mountains stood linked
In waves like camel humps dominating
Basin-crouched cities and plains.
Stubborn indices of continental drift,
Geographical collisions and bedrock are
testimonies that earth requires her own text,
That she too writes history in blood.

III
An orgasm of death entered Port-au-Prince
From the south, conquering a line of feeble towns.
Hopes granulated in an extended corridor
Of crushed bodies as a urinal of despots flushed
Into silence. Innocence is sliced by poverty.
Listen. The great baron's blades are sharpened.

IV
Tumbling and caving rocks brokered bustling
Streets into a morbid stillness. Port-au-Prince gagged
On dust spewed by the encroaching reaper-apocalypse.
Time oozed by as brave Haitians froze upon the sight
Of an instant masquerade and macabre carnival.
Spirits floated as thousands were snatched
By unannounced cherubins train-wrecking the earth.

V
Basin-filled cities and provinces became
Begging bowls still cuffed to 1804.
Despite hunger and expectations of mayhem,
Thousands of embattled bodies vigorously sang
To the cosmos refusing to partake in a dance
Macabre. Aid delivery charades and dignitary parades.

VI
We know the roads and we know the ropes,
Still cuffed to the beacon of 1804's maroons
We are swimming upstream against forceful
Tides of history, calamities and ravenous eagles.
Repeatedly clawed, our bodies, scaled with miseries
And now caught in an NGOs undertow.

VII

After two hundred and six years of desperate strokes,
Nature broke us. Now, there's a parade of vultures
Decked in full regalia on our shores. We are meat.
With punctured ribs and collapsed lungs, our gills
Are pried further open as our seasoned substance
Is wheedled and herded onto pristine marble slabs.
Despite resilience, we await the plunging predators' beak.

The Coffin Maker & The Poet

For Jacques Roche

Together:
We are from a flogging island
Where gusting winds turn dreams
Into dust and tattered houses kneel
Upon rocky hills, imploring
The desolate land. Tomb-like
Abodes stud the city, and nailing
Shut disfigured dreams.
As tyrannical waves flog the island,
We hope for an affable rhythm.

Coffin Maker:
I've watched you perambulate
With confident steps and wondered about
Your height. I want your dreams to repose
Within a receptacle made of cedar and pine.
You are a peacock in your bearing,
And your exit from this land must pass
Through my workshop. Splendid and
Crafted, witnessed by the nostalgic.
But if I depart first, pen me a poem.

The Poet:
I've walked by your shop, drawn to
Fresh scent of poplar, pine & cedar.
The whirring music of your saws hum
To my probing ears. I wonder about the dead trees.
Our mountains are barren; our lives romped
By the riotous orgy of disorder, a macabre dance
Burying hopes in coffin coffers. Ominous hearses,
Funeral-carnivals clamor in the streets.
You have grown muscular from sawing
Trees that beg not to be turned into coffins.

Coffin Maker:
Poet dreamer, you walk among trees
And do you not pen your poems on flesh?
The trees too cried as they turned into paper.
Perhaps the shark-like teeth of my chisel
And whirring sounds of iron slicing through
Wood bleed ears, but your pen is
A blade too. Sharp, unforgiving, a social dagger.
Some in this city burn under your pen's fire
Refusing to fix their out-of-step dance,
Your piquant lines are the peoples' tunes.

The Poet:
We are the people my friend. You build
Our wooden boxes of permanent dormancy;
I scribble the whaling sounds of the land
That burn my pen into an amber metal,

Glowing on our charred roads. Ravaged
Memories implode in the trappings of needs.
Time is unforgiving in this cramped island
Where blood-binging tyrants make the coffin
Makers consume more trees than poets.
Your sawdust will not obstruct my voice.

Coffin Maker:
My sawdust will not filch the beaming aura
Of your gaze, nor suffuse the morning dew
Of your voice. You must recite your poem
About the dog that gulped poverty while dreaming
Of his old broth plate. We escape through your words,
And our eardrums make us dance to your rhythm.
Swaying as if in a meditative state, we hang to the edges
Of your words. In this terrestrial darkness
You are a sunbeam and no dust can cloud your light.

The Poet:
I dreamt I was swaddled in one of your coffins.
Mourners gathered in front of your shop like
A chapel. Twisted cotton meshes burned
In orange-peel halves filled with palm oil,
As mass was said by a disfigured priest holding
A black book. He took elliptical breaths between
The lines, disrupting the cadences. Fire sputtered
Through eyes carving my name on lacquered
Cedar. Our crying forest has been ditched by tyrannical
Waves. Hacked planks beg in this saw-buzzing kingdom.

Coffin Maker:
In this kingdom, this barren land of bones, convulsion
Is the rhythm. Dust gags dreams. Rags gag poets.
Crying becomes ritual as poetry is to eulogy,
And coffins are to funerals. I chisel my art on coffers
of last rites, a planetarium of one's own, so dignity,
The last possession can be protected from maggots.
I apologize for the trees, but death is the rhythm
Of tyrants and its racket pervades disconsolate borders.
Lives are unhinged doors and broken twigs. Soundproof
Coffins are sealants for gutted and mutilated humanities.

The Poet:
In a kingdom of chaos where rocks and bullets are
Shooting stars, the poet's pen is not the magic wand
That will stop the eternal unraveling of lives. I've tried
To pen dreams into structures, but my ink bled. This
Is the avalanche of despair where ribs crack as twigs
Under the weight of boots. Broken, unhinged, crumpled.
In this terrestrial darkness, my friend, you bequeathed
Me a sunbeam and now no dust can cloud my light. I am
The moving target of advancing dictators. I fear my dreams.
Newly constructed doors become stretchers. Bloodied,
Cadavers pass through crowded streets without sirens.

Together:
We are from a flogging island where gusting winds
Turn dreams into dust and tattered houses kneel
Upon rocky hills, imploring the desolate land.

Tomb-like abodes stud the city, nailing shut
Disfigured dreams. As tyrannical waves flog the island,
Like whales, we moan for this land.

Coffin Maker:
In the shadow of a moonless July night, a star was netted,
Chained and handcuffed to a chair. We waited four days
In the dark until we knew your eyes would no longer reflect
The sun. My poet friend, my orbit is now unbalanced
In this chaotic kingdom. They left you without
Your rhythmical tongue and shackled you with a rusted chain.
Your hand swelled behind your back as you were dumped
Shirtless and shoeless on the hot pavement. Your blue
Shorts glistened beside a pool, as an island of blood
Trailed from your head. The earth convulsed.

A State of Encounter

After Roxane Gay's novel An Untamed State

A tropical vortex thrashed you within a cage.
You hung by the bones like a fish stinking
in its slow death. No water, just a forest
of hurt. *Homo erectus* slow-knifing you
into a primal state. Grunting for the dark
cloak of Hades in the stead of Persephone's
crown. You had already consummated with a wrestler,
a farm boy-turned-engineer you wish to forget.

Forgetting cannot be unlooped when golden
alliances enter the body via the indexing
of promises. A scar-faced commander desired
you for eternity, an extension of his violent will.
Your refusal charged his caliber as he pulped you
into craved submission. But your will graved its own
vault, your body endured the quakes, knowing
the battled field will have to bury its own ghosts.

Fracas. Your caged state shattered shutters of pearl
in the *before*. The children of L'Ouverture were palm
fronds, fronding lights onto the world of flesh traders.
Now, darkness radiates from a once clement Caribbean
Camelot. A claimant, a lore-ranting charlatan of love,
a breaker, a lorry-of-a-commander who muddies potential.
Zeus, in your hungry, angry land. With dews of light
broken, you consumed Persephone's pomegranate seeds.

Bars of the old cage rodded your spine, you returned
to Hades, quaking under the bulk of darkness
until your skin grew layers of steel. The leash dropped.
Your gaze hardened, your father's epaulettes altered into feathers.
His pride plummeted from their pillars. Elated, you flew back
to the sunshine state. At an eatery, the scar-faced commander
served water. Trembling. Like a charged rod, you cleft his darkness,
and swallowed the Aurora Borealis gleaming your being with light.

An Unimmaculate State

After Marlon James' short story "Immaculate"

The body arrived like a spring roll in a Moroccan carpet.
Her feet, bare, would have to gargle humiliation
A thousand times before ogling the geometric
Eloquence of Berber wool. Instead, the pounded
Floor of her zinc-roofed shack blares paucity.

In this part of town, poverty spins like a propeller.
Debasement blows below the immaculate girls'
Folds. Averted eyes, eyes averted, the ways of bumping
And grinding on minors. Minor scales. Scaling worth.
Mouths muted by needs and fear. Reticence for sale.

Silence appeared in large unnamed registered envelopes.
Tears sponged with thousands of crisp notes, and grievances
Breathe greener air. New dress, shoes, a spot in Dovecot
Cemetery, where elites' remains remain in segregated
Hordes, hoarding like Pharaohs uptown, posh to the bones.

Someone, perhaps two, boned Jacqueline Stenton
Until her fifteen year-old eyes fossilized into amber.
The ruby red Saab and white Land Rover roamed
Her fancy Trenchtown dreams, transacting her *punany*
For uptown favors as her back bore the recompense.

Alicia Mowatt knows that in the world of monsters, there is
No quittance. Nightmares are rooted in emblems. The ruby
Red Saab at the cemetery parked at a distance. A student
Who scaled the walls of class with Jacqueline, stepped out.
Melissa Cleo's Immaculate uniform is pleated in silence.

Substance

In memory of FC

A light dimmed, a clement element vanished,
The farming flags of sovereignty fly half-mast,

And rivulets of tears became tributaries for constellations
Of hope. What you fed the paupers of this world lingers

In the bloodstream like a serum for revival, a downhome
Chicken broth, or an oxtail stew making dreams flex.

You were a clement farmer who denied clemency to
Devourers of canes who pulped lives in fields.

You can never be silenced since your history is not reticent,
And you move like an ever flowing current; a sustaining

Substance as significant as a meal from the first harvest,
And as poignant as our doting gaze on a newfangled lighthouse.

Howling Wind

In our pounded earth-room
Painted blue, we encounter
The blues of the tropic—sorrow
Wrapped in a single bed sheet,
Double limbed—sweating as the wind
Winds and loops fear between our fingers.
My hands register the howling wind
As if blown through a conch shell, or a trumpet
Bemoaning the blues through depressed
Valves. The sea grows horns, turning
Into thousands of raging bulls stabbing
Southern coastal towns, where paupers' homes
Become graveyards without headstones.

We have joined the ranks of the homeless,
Thousands like us, exposed vines entangled
Ashore as hopes sail away with the dusk.
Hurricane Matthew broke spines already fractured,
Stooping us to the level of canines, howling.
We were unprepared for this storm,
Whose eyes roamed like a jet, fueling despair
With each twist and twitch, plantations
Emptying their crops as proffers to the Mayan god,
Huracán. No appeasement, no acceptance.
The K'iche' tongue of Huracán could not be deciphered.
Half a million people weighed down by water,
Leaving their malaise behind as death sheds tears
For the sheer number of unknown and unclaimed bodies.

ACKNOWLEDGMENTS & GRATITUDE

Grateful to the editors of the publications in which the following poems, or versions of them, have appeared:

"Granulated Hopes," *Anchor Literary Magazine*.

"A Palace of Mourners," *Calabash: A Journal of Caribbean Arts & Letters*.

"Century of Ashes, and Catacomb," *PBS NewsHour*.

"A Naked State" *SpoKe 5*.

"Survey at Body #33," *SX Salon*.

"The Coffin Maker & The Poet," *Transition*.

I would like to extend a special thanks to my wife and close friend, Jalene, for her support and always my first reader. I would also like to thank Enzo Silon Surin for his gracious invitation to be a part of the Central Square Press family; Danielle Legros-George for her friendship and support. Thanks to: Sandy Alexandre, Tina Beyene, Kevin Gallagher, Yusef Komunyakaa, Robert Pinsky, Jenny Factor, Djeunie Saint-Louis, Gina Désir, Jean-Dany Joachim, Edwidge Danticat, Marie-Maude Evans, Faith Smith, Sandra McCollin, my mother Bernadette, and all of my in-laws for their support. Also, to my traveling guides as I continue to journey in this world.

ABOUT THE AUTHOR

Patrick Sylvain is a poet, writer, social critic, photographer and the author of the chapbook UNDERWORLDS (Central Square Press, 2018). Twice nominated for the Pushcart Prize, his work has also been published in several scholarly and creative journals and anthologies. Sylvain holds an Ed.M. from Harvard University and an MFA from Boston University (Robert Pinsky Global Fellow) and serves on the faculty at Brown University. Sylvain is also the Shirle Dorothy Robbins Creative Writing Prize Fellow at Brandeis University and has a collection of essays, forthcoming from Beacon Press in 2019.

Other titles from Central Square Press

A HARD SUMMATION by Afaa Michael Weaver (2014)

CRACKED CALABASH by Lisa Pegram (2015)

THE NEXT VERSE POETS MIXTAPE - VOLUME ONE: THE 4 x 4 by Melanie Henderson, Fred Joiner, Lisa Pegram, Enzo Silon Surin (2016)

FEAR OF DOGS & OTHER ANIMALS by Shauna M. Morgan (2016)

A LETTER OF RESIGNATION: AN AMERICAN LIBRETTO (2017) by Enzo Silon Surin

LETTERS FROM CONGO by Danielle Legros Georges (2017)

DEPARTURE by Samuel Miranda (2017)

www.ingramcontent.com/pod-product-compliance
Lightning Source LLC
Chambersburg PA
CBHW071758080526
44588CB00013B/2296